CUSTOM SNEAKERS

EVERYTHING YOU NEED TO PERSONALIZE YOUR KICKS

KNZ (@KNZ.TV)

Photography by Alexi Pav

CONTENTS

01. INTRODUCTION

What Does Customizing Sneakers Mean?	9
The History of Custom Sneakers	10
Choosing Your Sneakers	14
5 Emblematic Models	17
Supplies	30
Essential Steps	36
Brainstorming	37
Making Your Sneakers in Three Steps	40
Anatomy of a Sneaker	42

02. TECHNIQUES

Painting on Fabric	48
Masking Your Shoe	49
Unstitching a Logo	52
Making Stencils	54
Drawing without Knowing How to Draw	57
Flat Surfaces	59
Making a Splash	61
Making a "Marble" Effect	65
Dyeing with Coffee	66
Painting with a Toothpick	68
Customizing with Accessories	70

03. CUSTOMS

Nike Air Force 1 "Energy"	74
Converse Chuck Taylor All Star "Graffiti"	84
Adidas Stan Smith "Flower"	92
Air Jordan 1 "Cartoon"	100
New Balance 574 "Color"	110

04. BONUS

Tools to Dig Deeper	120
Taking Care of Your Custom Sneakers over Time	122
The Impact of Custom Sneakers on Fashion	124
SOS KNZ: I Have a Problem with My Custom Sneaker!	128
Inspirations	130
Glossary	136
Mockups for Your Custom Sneakers	137

YO ARTISTS !

If you already know me, it isn't too weird to meet up here again, right? The first thing I want to do is dedicate this book to you, because it's thanks to you that I've been able to go from YouTube to TikTok to writing a book! So while I can't say it enough, thank you.

But if you don't know me yet.... Hey there, I'm Kenza, aka Knz. Like most little kids, once I had a pencil in my hand, I started drawing. I guess I got into it a little too much, because then I moved on from drawing to crafts, origami, clay sculptures, and watercolors! I've always had a lot of creative curiosity, and one day in 2012, it led me to Google Images, looking at a photo of a young woman customizing a pair of Timberland Boots Originals. I fell in love with customizing sneakers right away, because two of my passions from then had appeared before my eyes: drawing and sneakers. I customized my first pair of sneakers soon afterward—two pairs of Adidas belonging to my little brother, who was still a baby. At the time, I had no idea that almost 15 years later, it would become my career and I'd write a book about the subject.

It's true that I may not be the most experienced or best custom artist around, but ever since I started, I've always tried to improve, share this world with others, and pay more and more attention to my clients' requests.

So there you have it. I wanted to collect all the information in one place to let anyone easily customize their sneakers. And let me stop you right now: You don't need to know how to draw. Customizing is just adding your personal touch. And you'll see that there are lots of ways to do it. But customizing is also a culture with loads of stories to share.

In *Custom Sneakers*, I'll take you into this world that I find so fascinating—and I hope I'll be able to fascinate you (at least a little) in turn.

INTRODUCTION

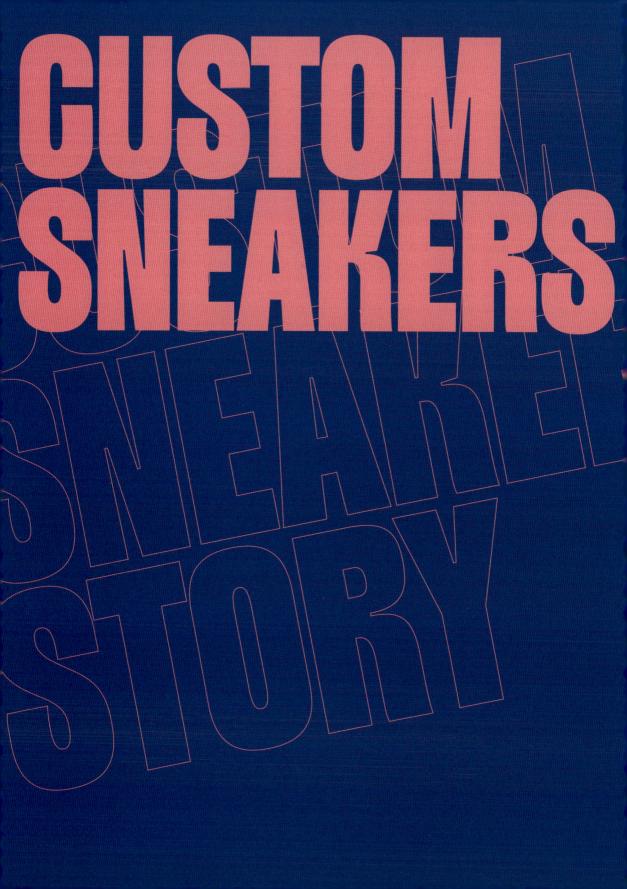

WHAT DOES CUSTOMIZING SNEAKERS MEAN?

Before telling you how to customize your own sneakers, I think I should explain what I'm talking about!

Customizing sneakers is a practice with the goal of personalizing a pair of shoes via a set of techniques and methods.

The name of the practice is a mixture of several terms—and for good reason! The word "custom" comes from the word "customization," which means "personalization." So whether you hear "customization"—a custom sneaker, not a custom or habit—or "personalization," all these words refer to the same thing. The word "sneakers," of course, means a pair of athletic shoes worn in daily city life.

CUSTOMIZING: A COMBINATION OF TECHNIQUES

Contrary to what many people think, customizing your shoes involves more than painting them. And you don't need to be able to draw! There are lots of techniques that let you modify and personalize your sneakers: using markers, sewing, adding accessories, and even tattooing them (really, really—I promise!). Truth be told, there isn't a hard-and-fast rule that limits the possible techniques you can use. Some have proved their worth over a number of years. But every artist tends to develop their own techniques. It's totally fascinating!

A SHOE OR A WORK OF ART?

Originally, custom sneakers were intended to be worn, so the techniques had to be durable enough that they wouldn't disintegrate after the first step outside.

But with the sneakerhead cult that has developed around sneakers over the past few decades, they've become collectors' items desired in their own right, giving rise to custom sneakers that are more artistic than functional. As part of this, there are even techniques specifically made for custom sneakers that are intended for display.

EXPRESS YOURSELF WITH CUSTOM SNEAKERS!

As I said earlier, there are many techniques for modifying and personalizing your sneakers. In this book I'm going to cover just some of the vast options for customizing them. I'll only show you painting techniques that use a paintbrush and also accessories that you'll readily have at home. I've adapted all the techniques so that you can wear your shoes.

Custom Sneakers is, first and foremost, my view of customizing sneakers, but there are as many ways of making them as there are people who do it! What I like most about custom sneakers is how we can use them to express ourselves and to communicate with other people. For me, a good custom sneaker tells a story.

It's up to you to decide what story you'll tell with your sneakers.

INTRODUCTION

INTRODUCTION

THE HISTORY OF CUSTOM SNEAKERS

Where do custom sneakers come from... or, rather, what culture are they from? I grew up surrounded by this culture, and I can't imagine writing a book about custom sneakers without sharing a little of their wonderful story with you!

Customizing your sneakers isn't new. From a kid scribbling on their pair of Converse shoes to a skater tagging their Vans, personalizing by hand is as old as selling sneakers.

But as a culture—because, yes, it is a culture—customizing is closely linked to sneakers. To understand both of them, we have to go back to mid-1970s New York, in the Bronx. That's where a cultural movement that would shake up society around the world was born, affecting everything from music to dance by way of shoes: hip-hop!

B-BOYS AND HIP-HOP

Hip-hop culture began in the streets, within the Black and Latinx communities. Many art practices surround the movement, such as DJing, graffiti, breakdancing, and, the most popular of all of them, rap.

Breakdancers, called "B-boys" ("break-boys"), were the first to wear athletic shoes off the basketball court. For them, sneakers were the best type of shoes for their art. They liked to wear Puma Clydes or even Adidas Superstars. B-boys converted them from their original purpose as sports equipment and used them for performing, and they made them the centerpiece of their outfits. So, yes, if basketball is where the craze for sneakers began, hip-hop is indeed what made them into a real style accessory.

Little by little, B-boys created a lifestyle and sense of coolness around sneakers that made them popular, turning them into a street item that belonged to hip-hop in their own right!

Hip-hop came into being in a socioeconomic context marked by stigmatizing the Black and Latinx populations. So in response to that scorn, its fans used their culture as a way to affirm and express themselves in a society that rejected them. This is what B-boys did via outfits that let them express themselves and proclaim their style and their world. Their sneakers were the final touch to their outfits, which was why they had to be as clean as possible. A real obsession for cleanliness arose from this. Plus, when you lack resources, you can't throw out your sneakers after they get their first scratch. Instead, you have to take good care of them. With a toothbrush behind the ear, B-boys were always ready to erase the tiniest mark as soon as their sneakers rubbed the sidewalk a bit. And to stand out even more, what's better than customizing your sneakers? Hence the appearance of big or colored laces that let you be much more visible.

INTRODUCTION

Members of the rap group Run-DMC. Left to right: Jason Mizell (Jam Master Jay), Darryl McDaniels (DMC), and Joseph Simmons (Rev Run).

THE SNEAKERS EXPLOSION

In 1983, a new group entered the scene, the first musical group to be sponsored by an athletic shoe brand, Adidas. That group was Run-DMC, three rappers who decided to wear their street "look" onstage. Dressed in leather jackets, fedoras, and black pants and with Adidas on their feet, the group went against the style of Black singers of the time completely, choosing more of a funk look. Since some people viewed them negatively, they decided to rap loudly and clearly about their way of life in a song that later became a hit, "My Adidas," referring to the Adidas Superstar model that rappers everywhere wore. Their fans went wild for them and bought Adidas Superstars en masse. Adidas picked up on the craze and was forced to recognize the group's unprecedented impact on sales, signing a million-dollar contract sponsoring Run-DMC.

Building from this exposure and the artist-brand collaboration that Run-DMC had launched, the popularity of sneakers kept growing, reaching another turning point with the arrival of Michael Jordan at Nike. In 1985, Nike, which had been on the sidelines of the sneaker market at the time, decided to release a new athletic shoe model, the Air Jordan 1 High. Thanks to Michael Jordan's talent and popularity, as well as bold ad campaigns, Air Jordan 1 Highs soon were a resounding success, becoming must-have items.

michael jordan

In the early 1990s, sneakers were officially fashionable.

CUSTOM SNEAKERS AND HIP-HOP CULTURE

Going back again for a moment, let's head to early 1980s Harlem, New York. The boutique of Dapper Dan, who designed his own clothes, was popular with dealers who wanted to show off their wealth via their outfits. At his customers' request, Dan added luxury brand logos and monograms to customize their clothing. Let's be clear here: this is illegal—it's called counterfeiting—but that was just one more aspect that made his customers like it. Finally, the entire essence of the customizing culture had coalesced: appropriating an item and then expressing yourself with what you have on hand. When the new hip-hop culture exploded and rappers also started to earn money, they went to Dapper Dan to imitate gangster style. His boutique quickly became the hot meeting place for the New York hip-hop scene. Beyond clothing, the designer also worked on his clients' sneakers, including Nike and New Balance. To match the shoes to the rappers' outfits, he attached canvas decorated with Gucci or Louis Vuitton monograms. He was a real trailblazer!

Storefront of Dapper Dan's boutique in the 1980s.

ZOOM IN ON

ADIDAS MARKERS AT THE HEART OF CUSTOM CULTURE

Adidas clearly understood the idea of standing out by customizing your shoes! In 1983, the brand sold an all-white sneaker that came with a set of Adicolor markers for customizing the shoes. What did the ads promise? Special quick-drying, waterproof markers for Adidas athletic shoes—markers that are no longer marketed in 2025!

Today's entire customization and sneaker market shows the legacy of hip-hop because that is the culture that popularized the shoes. But the art of customizing doesn't completely belong to them. Personalizing our belongings is a spontaneous act that turns up elsewhere. For example:

• Kurt Cobain wrote "Endorsement" on the toe box of his Converse. Scribbling on your shoes was totally part of grunge culture.
• In 1966, long before the birth of hip-hop, the Vans brand essentially sold bespoke models at its customers' request.

CHOOSING YOUR SNEAKERS

There are a number of criteria that can help you choose which sneakers to customize, specifically, the material and the style.

01

MATERIAL

The first thing to look at is the material the sneakers are made of. You can paint on almost any material with the right products. The fine print is that some materials are easier to work with than others. The easiest ones are leather (or faux leather) and fabric, which is lucky, because paint stands up the best on these materials and they're also commonly used in manufacturing athletic shoes. Brands that specialize in customizing sell paints made for leather; these can also work on fabric, with additives or water to make them flow better. By extension, these brands also sell additives so that you can apply their paints to other materials, such as plastic or latex.

If you don't have much experience, I recommend that you opt for leather or fabric shoes and that you don't mix too many materials.

02

STYLE

High-tops, low-tops, Velcro, or laces . . . first and foremost, what really matters most is that you like the sneakers. But some shapes will make your work easier than others. So if you're a beginner, choose a clean, simple sneaker style.

INTRODUCTION

ZOOM IN ON

LEATHER OR FAUX?

Most "leather" sneakers are actually faux leather. Less expensive than the real thing, faux leather is a fabric that imitates leather perfectly. It consists of a front that looks like leather and a woven canvas backing. In this book, I'll use the words "leather" and "faux leather" interchangeably to refer to shoes that look like leather.

I recommend you pick a smooth leather, as paint will adhere to it better.

PROS AND CONS OF LEATHER SHOES

+ You can wash your custom sneakers.
+ You can correct painting errors.
+ There are more leather sneaker models.
− There's a greater risk of the paint peeling or getting damaged.

FABRIC

I recommend you choose Converse or Vans shoes made of all canvas.

PROS AND CONS OF FABRIC SHOES

+ They don't require prep or finish steps.
+ The paint adheres and lasts better.
+ They are compatible with more techniques.
− They are hard to wash.
− It's harder to correct painting errors.

INTRODUCTION

5 EMBLEMATIC MODELS

IN *CUSTOM SNEAKERS*, I'VE CHOSEN FIVE EMBLEMATIC MODELS TO GUIDE YOU AS YOU LEARN ABOUT CUSTOMIZING.

↘

INTRODUCTION

[01] # ICONIC
NIKE AIR FORCE 1
CUSTOM ARTISTS' FAVORITE CANVAS

I was taken aback to learn that the first people to customize their Air Force 1s were NY dealers in the 1980s. Designed by Bruce Kilgore, the Air Force 1 first appeared in 1982 in a high-top version, the Nike Air Force 1 High. It quickly attracted its intended buyers, basketball players, thanks to a bubble of air built into the sole, which provided improved cushioning on the court. This was the first model to incorporate Nike's "Air" technology, which they have since made a household name with other emblematic models such as the Air Jordan and Air Max. Surprisingly, this wasn't at all the pair of shoes Nike had planned at the beginning, so much so that they took it off the market in 1984 and 1985. When Nike released it again, it quickly caught the attention of dealers, who saw it as the perfect shoe to match their extravagant outfits. To do so, they needed to customize the shoe a bit, give it some color—and with its simple lines and full white look, the Air Force was the perfect canvas to take on all colors. The shoes reached an unprecedented level of popularity when 1990s and 2000s rappers latched onto them, inspired by the gangster and street style they'd grown up with.

WHY CHOOSE IT TO CUSTOMIZE?

✛ All leather = easier to paint on a shoe made of only one material.
✛ Completely white original model.
✛ Divided into sections = helps with placement.
✛ Goes with almost all outfits.
✛ There are lots of custom sneakers out there already to inspire you.

INTRODUCTION

INTRODUCTION

02 MYTHIC
AIR JORDAN 1 HIGH

THE MODEL THAT PROPELLED NIKE TO NUMBER 1 AND TOOK THE SNEAKER CULT TO NEW HEIGHTS

What a story! In 1984, Nike struggled to find a place in the market, behind Reebok and Converse. As the "white-class brand," the company suffered from low sales, as it lacked credibility both in basketball and on the street. That's when Nike decided to bet the house on a certain Michael Jordan and market a model under his name, just as he was taking his first steps in the NBA. Thanks to the talent of Jordan, who ran circles around his opponents every game; the funny, daring ad campaigns that spotlighted young players' rebellious sides; and the shoes, which didn't conform to the NBA's uniform rules, the Air Jordan 1 High was quickly established as popular among connoisseurs and neophytes. Two versions came out in rapid succession, the Air Jordan Mid and the Air Jordan Low. In the early 1990s, they were such a big craze that one American in 12 had at least one pair of Jordans. It was official: sneakers and sportswear were fashionable.

INTRODUCTION

WHY CHOOSE IT TO CUSTOMIZE?

+ All leather = easier to paint on a shoe made of only one material.
+ Available in white.
+ Large surface area in the Mid and High versions = more room to paint.
+ Divided into parts = helps with placement.

INTRODUCTION

[03]
CLASSIC
ADIDAS STAN SMITH

THE TWICE-BORN MODEL

In my opinion, all those people who walk around with the face of a guy with a mustache on the tongue of their Adidas Stan Smiths without knowing who he is are pretty funny. And that's exactly who the model is named for: 1970s star tennis player Stan Smith. Even funnier is that another player, named Robert Haillet, originally represented the model. But Haillet saw his signature—then affixed to the outer uppers—gradually give way to Smith's growing fame. In 1978, all traces of Haillet completely disappeared from the shoes, which were officially renamed Adidas Stan Smiths. Sales of the already popular shoe climbed under its new name and with this new face. Overtaken in the 1980s by more successful models, Stan Smiths were no longer a feature on the tennis court, appearing instead on the feet of a public that ranged from fans of hip-hop to hooligans. The popularity of the model changed dramatically in 2012 when the directors of Adidas took their flagship model completely off the market, creating confusion, frustration, and, above all, demand among customers. In 2014, when the company announced the return of the shoes, they were a big hit. Stan Smiths became a permanent fixture among the emblematic models of sneakers and pop culture for a generation that probably didn't know that a successful tennis pro was hiding behind their shoes.

WHY CHOOSE IT TO CUSTOMIZE?

+ All leather = easier to paint on a shoe made of only one material.
+ Completely white original model.
+ Large surface area in the Mid and High versions = more room to paint.
+ No insets or seams = it's harder to draw over seams and insets.

04

VINTAGE
CONVERSE CHUCK TAYLOR ALL STAR

THE MODEL WITH THE MOST DIVERSE, WILDEST FASHION TRENDS

Did you know that when this model began in 1917, it wasn't called Converse Chuck Taylor All Star, and it didn't have a star on its patch either? In the early 1920s, basketball player Charles "Chuck" Taylor popularized the model. To thank him for contributing to the brand's rise, Converse added "Chuck Taylor" between two points of the star on the "All Star" patch glued on the inside of the ankle of the shoe. Thus Converse's emblematic model was born. Over the years, basketball turned away from the model in favor of leather shoes, which are better suited to the sport. The emergence of Nike and its new models pushed Converse into the background, but against all expectations, Chuck Taylors took hold in other cultures. Characterized by a rebellious spirit, the music industry's counterculture—such as punk rock and grunge—started to adopt Chuck Taylor All Stars. A number of celebrities wore them, from Elvis Presley to Snoop Dogg and from the members of Nirvana to even Sylvester Stallone in *Rocky 2*. Made popular by big names in art, fashion, and sports, and for the attitude they exemplify, the Chuck Taylor All Star has become a fashion icon.

WHY CHOOSE IT TO CUSTOMIZE?

✦ Large surface area = more room to paint.
✦ Fabric = no prep or finish steps.
✦ No insets or seams = it's harder to draw over seams and insets.

INTRODUCTION

INTRODUCTION

[05] **RESTYLED
NEW BALANCE 574**

COMFORT FIRST

I love the fact that when William J. Riley founded this brand in 1906, his only ambition was to come up with orthotic soles. It was only much later that New Balance marketed its very first running shoe, gradually expanding its product range with specialized shoes for tennis, boxing, and baseball. But up to the 2010s, the brand struggled to break free from its neutral image, as its color scheme often centered on gray and its promotional campaigns focused on the practical. Buying New Balance meant buying good-quality shoes that were certainly very comfortable and well priced but lacked a cool attitude. This changed in 2017 with the "dad shoes" trend, followed by a series of collaborations with the fashion houses Casablanca and Aimé Leon Dore and also the designer Salehe Bembury, who presented models with a fresher, more colorful look. The New Balance 574 was originally designed as a running shoe, but it quickly became a versatile, classic lifestyle model.

WHY CHOOSE IT TO CUSTOMIZE?

+ Suede = a specific way of finishing leather that gives it a velvety appearance and is soft to the touch. No prep or finish steps.

+ Divided into parts – helps with placement.

INTRODUCTION

OTHER IDEAS FOR MODELS...

NIKE BLAZER MID '77

✛ Equivalent to a Converse Chuck Taylor All Star in leather.

VANS SLIP-ONS

+ Large fabric surface area
+ Divided into several parts

TIMBERLAND YELLOW BOOT

+ (Very) large suede surface area
+ Divided into several parts

NIKE DUNK LOW

+ All leather
+ Divided into several parts

ADIDAS SUPERSTAR

+ Leather upper

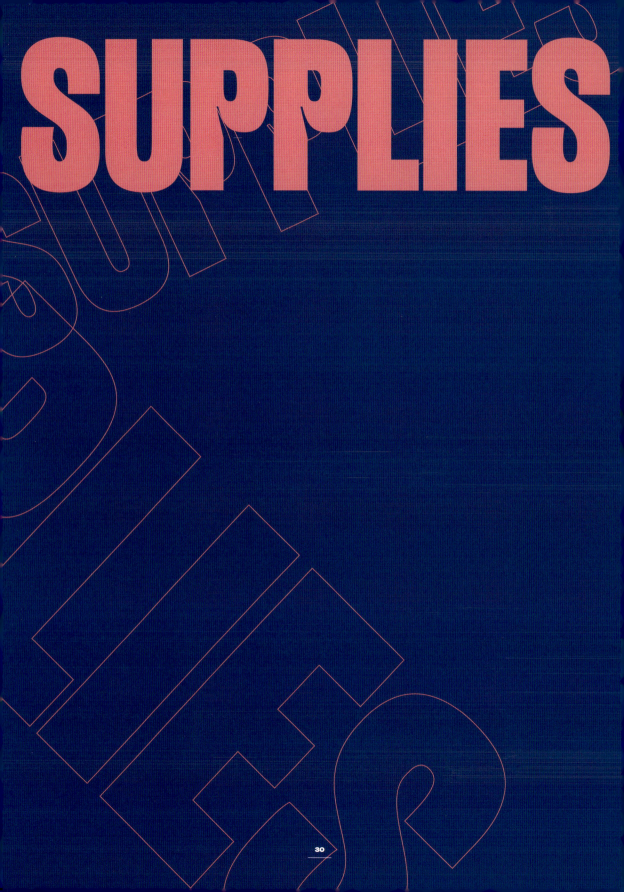

INTRODUCTION

SPECIALIZED
SUPPLIES

LOOK NO MORE! In this section you'll find all the supplies you'll need to create your custom sneakers.

PAINTS

There aren't many paints made for customizing sneakers. Of these, the best known, which I use, are:

• Angelus paints: water- and silicone-based, they're elastic and protective. So they're perfect for customizing on leather; they can be used on fabric when mixed with water or with an additive to make them more liquid.

• Pébéo Setacolor leather paints: this is a line of durable acrylic paints with good coverage, developed for leather and faux leather.

• Most acrylic paints you find in a store aren't suitable for customizing.

GET IN THE HABIT: TAKING CARE OF YOUR BRUSHES

• While you're working: clean in water immediately.

• Once you're done: clean under a warm stream of water, with Marseille soap.

TIP

A well-cleaned brush has no paint residue on its bristles.

BRUSHES

A paintbrush is an extension of your hand. While using it requires some skill, with practice it's a tool that you'll be able to master with no problem.

What's cool about paintbrushes is that you don't have to invest in expensive major brands. The ones that give you the best for the money and that I recommend are:

• Synthetic Leonard Blue Line brushes

• Synthetic Rougier & Plié brushes: depending on what you want to paint, they sell the appropriate brush shape:

• Flat paintbrushes for flat surfaces

• Round and fine paintbrushes for contours and details

INTRODUCTION

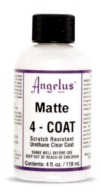

SOLVENTS

These products are essential but must be used with care. They're chemicals that let you clean the leather before painting on it. They dissolve and get rid of all residues that might interfere with applying paint, such as varnish, silicone, or dirt.

•Angelus sells its own solvent, Angelus Preparer and Deglazer.
•Acetone

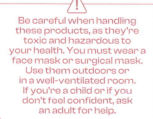

Be careful when handling these products, as they're toxic and hazardous to your health. You must wear a face mask or surgical mask. Use them outdoors or in a well-ventilated room. If you're a child or if you don't feel confident, ask an adult for help.

VARNISHES

Paint brands specialized for customizing generally sell specialized varnishes:

•Angelus varnishes
•Pébéo Setacolor varnishes

Most varnishes you find in a store aren't suitable for customizing.

Depending on the finish you want to give your custom sneakers, you can choose between:

•matte
•satin
•glossy

MASKING TAPE

This is very useful for masking areas you don't want to paint without worrying about crossing into them. Depending on the area to be masked, you can use:

•paper tape
•vinyl tape

It's easy to find these tapes in the DIY section of a store, but most are too sticky and pull off the paint (which is a big pain). A little tip for avoiding this is to make the tape less sticky by applying it to a surface several times before using it on your shoes.

X-ACTO KNIFE
A very useful multifunctional tool that will let you unstitch a Swoosh and cut masking tape or other materials.

TRACING PAPER
This is the secret to reproducing any pattern or design!

FACE MASK
Consider protecting yourself by wearing a mask if you use a solvent:
- A face mask with a filter
- If you don't have a surgical mask, work in a well-ventilated room or outdoors.

PALETTE
You'll put your paints on this and use it to mix them.

INTRODUCTION

SUPPLIES FROM AROUND THE HOUSE

TOOTHPICKS
Handy for painting precise edges and scraping paint stains off soles.

COTTON PADS COTTON SWABS
These are useful for applying solvent on bigger or smaller areas.

PLASTIC TRAY
This is the perfect container for making your water- and coffee-based dyes! It needs to be big enough to hold two shoes, or get one for each.

SCISSORS
Always useful to have a pair handy.

TOOTHBRUSH
The perfect tool for making spots, splashes, or paint splatters.

INSTANT COFFEE
Instant coffee is an excellent natural dye. Mixed with warm water, it colors leather or plastic materials and is perfect for dyeing fabric.

GLOVES
Some custom artists swear by gloves, but if you ask me, I don't like how they feel all that much! On the other hand, they're useful for protecting your hands, for example, while dyeing your shoes with coffee.

TWEEZERS
These let you pull out pieces of thread caught in the material after unstitching a logo. Choose slanted metal tweezers to save time.

CLOTH
It's always useful to have a cloth, whether it's a towel or an old T-shirt, to clean and protect things! But be careful that it doesn't pill or leave threads.

NOT REQUIRED BUT EASIER WITH . . .

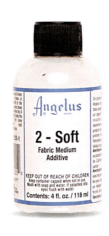

HEAT GUN
Originally used for DIY deglazing paint or varnish at high temperatures (200-600 C/392-1112°F), it can also be used to speed up paint drying. Put it about 20-30 cm (8-12 inches) from the surface you want to dry for several seconds.

⚠️ Be careful when using it to avoid getting burned, however.

ADDITIVES
These let paint work on materials other than leather (fabric, plastic, latex, etc.). In the beginning, you really will only need an additive that helps you make paint more liquid so that you can apply it on fabric.

Paint brands that specialize in customizing sneakers typically sell additives.

• Angelus Paints 2-Soft: mix it with your paint in a 1:1 ratio (50% paint, 50% 2-Soft) before applying it on your fabric. You can use water, but note that the ratio isn't the same. Only add a drop at a time and test it. Your paint shouldn't be too liquid.

INTRODUCTION

ESSENTIAL STEPS

I know all these steps can be frustrating and even scary at first glance. There are many steps to follow and products that are sometimes dangerous to handle, and it's a long process. But after you make two or three custom sneakers, the steps will become automatic, and you won't even have to think about them anymore!

BRAINSTORMING

WHY IS THIS IMPORTANT?

For me, brainstorming is the key to a successful custom sneaker. If you just want to add a little drawing or a simple touch of color, this step may not be necessary. But if you want to do something more complicated, I highly recommend you think about your custom sneaker before you dive in.

This process can be discouraging when you're starting, because as soon as your ideas begin to take seed, they start going in all directions. Focusing and selecting from your ideas is far from easy! But as with everything else, it's not a secret: practice helps you find your own ways of thinking.

TIP
Taking the time to really think about your custom sneaker saves you stress and time later on.

FINDING AN IDEA

Finding your idea means figuring out what you want to say with your custom sneaker. For me, custom sneakers tell us about things, and they can be anything: a film you want to pay tribute to, a memory that inspires you, an emotion you'd like to convey, a specific event—or just to make your shoes nicer. You can say what you want. So express yourself!

Your idea should be simple and clear. But just because an idea is simple, that doesn't mean producing it is easy. For example, you can start with a simple idea and then make it into a *full customization*, with many techniques involved.

To help with the process, tell yourself that your idea has to fit in one sentence. Think of it as a movie pitch, an overview of your creation.

TIP
To emphasize the concept of personalizing even more, name a pair based on its color scheme, collab, or type: doing this is very much following "sneaker culture" (e.g., Nike Dunk Low "Panda," Nike TN "Marseille," Nike Air Max 1 Patta "Monarch").

EXAMPLE

Let's take customizing a book as an example. If I summarized my ideas in one sentence, I'd say:

- For the Nike Air Force 1 "Energy": I saw a sweater with flames on it, and I thought it was super stylish! I want to make a custom sneaker inspired by it.

- For the New Balance 574 "Color": I don't like drawings all that much. I just want a colorful pair of shoes that are easy to wear.

- For the Converse Chuck Taylor All Star "Graffiti": I want shoes that are more personalized and that have a custom cool.

BRAINSTORMING (CONTINUED)

MOCKUP

The mockup comes between the idea and the custom sneaker.

Unlike a blank sheet of paper or canvas, the features of a shoe consist of its shapes, that is, its different parts, contours, etc. Thus, you can't customize two different shoes the same way: you have to adapt your customized design to the shapes of the shoe.

To design your custom sneaker, you'll need to make a mockup. Whether it's hand drawn or digitized, a mockup lets you test your ideas, try different versions, and move forward more calmly as you create.

Once you've made your mockup, you won't have to worry about the results of your customization anymore. You'll be able to focus exclusively on your technique.

TIP
Consider the specific shapes of the shoe to design your custom sneaker.

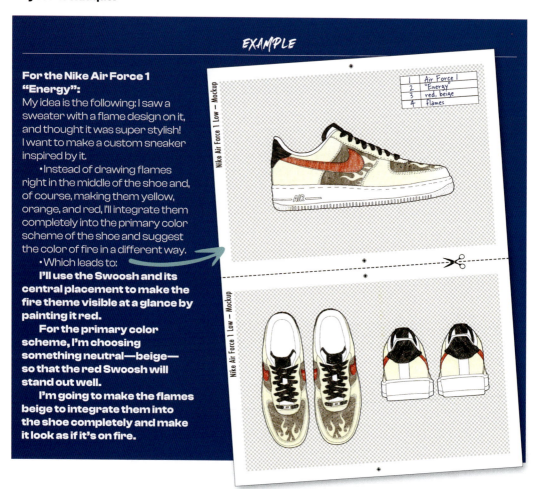

EXAMPLE

For the Nike Air Force 1 "Energy":
My idea is the following: I saw a sweater with a flame design on it, and thought it was super stylish! I want to make a custom sneaker inspired by it.
• Instead of drawing flames right in the middle of the shoe and, of course, making them yellow, orange, and red, I'll integrate them completely into the primary color scheme of the shoe and suggest the color of fire in a different way.
• Which leads to:
I'll use the Swoosh and its central placement to make the fire theme visible at a glance by painting it red.
For the primary color scheme, I'm choosing something neutral—beige—so that the red Swoosh will stand out well.
I'm going to make the flames beige to integrate them into the shoe completely and make it look as if it's on fire.

DRAWING YOUR MOCKUP

At the end of *Custom Sneakers*, you'll find a set of designs for a number of models of sneakers to help you make your own mockups on tracing paper. After you place the sheets of tracing paper over the models of the sneakers, you'll be able to draw directly on them and swap them around to create as many custom sneakers as you want without having to redraw the sneakers every time.

With this system, you'll be able to practice making your mockup as many times as you want, which will save time and let you keep track of your changes.

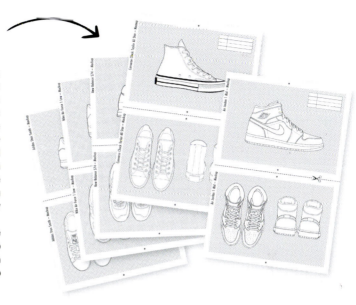

Nike Air Force 1 custom
Photoshop mockup

I HAVE A LITTLE PRESENT FOR YOU . . .

To make mockups that are even more realistic, go to my website at www.knz-custom.fr and download free digital mockups you can use in Photoshop. Download with the code PSDSNKRS. You don't have to be a Photoshop pro to use them! In a few clicks, you'll be able to change the color and add patterns or textures to your sneakers.

MAKING YOUR SNEAKERS IN THREE STEPS

The first time I painted a custom sneaker, I was so impatient to see the final result that I completely skipped some of the basic steps. My mistake? I didn't prep the leather that I was going to paint or varnish the paint I applied, which I regretted when the exterior paint flaked off in the midst of a photoshoot to immortalize my newly made custom sneaker! As you can see, these steps are crucial if you want your creation to last over time.

STEP 1

PREP
(leather only)

This step is only for leather shoes. Typically, new shoes made of leather have a varnish or industrial silicone finish coat. However, these products prevent paint from adhering to the leather properly.

Before applying any paint, therefore, you must deglaze the surfaces you're going to paint by rubbing them with solvent to get rid of the old industrial layer so the new coat of paint can stick.

Rub them with a cotton pad soaked with solvent (Angelus Preparer and Deglazer or acetone).

HOW DO I KNOW WHETHER I'VE PREPPED MY SURFACE PROPERLY?

Every model reacts to the prep step differently. On some, it will slightly damage the stitches and dissolve the leather coating a bit, but this isn't the case for all of them. (No worries if this happens with your model: it's normal.) To be sure you've done your prep step properly, use good products and rub well for at least 10 minutes.

Be careful when handling these products, however, as they're toxic and hazardous to your health. You must wear a face mask or surgical mask. Use them outdoors or in a well-ventilated room. If you're a child or if you don't feel confident, ask an adult for help. (It's nothing to be ashamed of!)

| STEP 2 | **PAINTING** |

You must always mix paint before using it. This makes the paint uniform. You should then apply it layer by layer until you get the color you want. Spread the paint well for each layer.

The layers must be very thin. Wait until the layer you just applied is dry before applying the next one. Drying time outdoors is 15 minutes plus or minus seconds with a heat gun.

| STEP 3 | **VARNISH** |
(leather only)

Varnish makes the final version of your design uniform and protects the paint. Apply two or three thin coats, letting each one dry between applications. Then let everything dry for 24 hours before handling it.

Be careful not to use the same paintbrush as the one you painted with!

TIP
Unlike leather, fabric doesn't need to be prepped before painting on it.

WHAT'S A GOOD CUSTOM SNEAKER?

To help me evaluate my custom sneakers I've put together a rubric with three criteria that let me judge a good custom design from a bad one:

• **Composition:**
how the elements of the composition are placed in relation to each other.

• **Design:**
how much the design looks like the original drawing.

• **Color:**
how well the colors go together and whether they're true to the original inspiration, if there was one.

INTRODUCTION

INTRODUCTION

ANATOMY
OF A SNEAKER

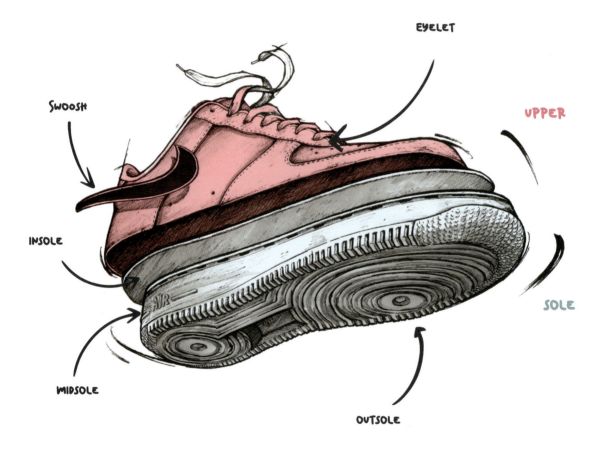

EYELET

SWOOSH

UPPER

INSOLE

SOLE

MIDSOLE

OUTSOLE

Note: Not all sneakers are made the same, but for the most part, the Nike Air Force 1 is a good example of the parts of a sneaker.

42

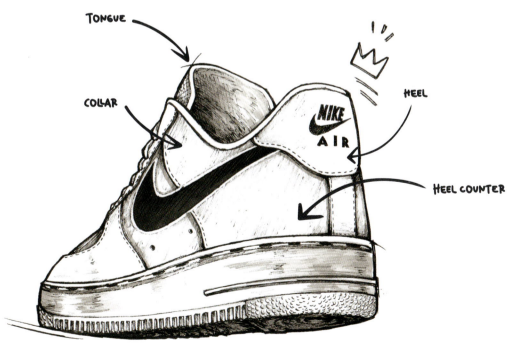

NOW IT'S YOUR TURN!

You are the crucial element in your creation. I know getting started is scary! You're afraid of ruining everything, plus it can be really discouraging when you don't like the results. But I promise it isn't really so bad if you mess up or aren't very good at the start. Put aside that negativity once and for all! You don't need it to create. Trust yourself—and if you already do, you're on the right path!

A few pieces of advice I'd like to share with you as you create: be patient, consider your progress, and try not to go too fast. Oh, yes, and last but not least, practice is the key!

I can't wait to see your creations! If you decide to post them on social media, I'd love to see them! Use #customsneakers, and don't forget to tag my account, @knz.tv.

TECHNIQUES

COME ON, LET'S PRACTICE! IN THIS CHAPTER, I'VE CHOSEN THE TECHNIQUES THAT I THINK ARE ESSENTIAL FOR STARTING OUT AND THAT WILL LET YOU WORK ON YOUR OWN. BUT I HOPE THIS CHAPTER WILL MAKE YOU WANT TO EXPERIMENT. THERE ARE THOUSANDS OF WAYS TO PERSONALIZE YOUR SHOES, SO AFTER LEARNING THE BASICS, IT'S UP TO YOU TO FIND YOUR OWN.

TECHNIQUES

PAINTING ON
FABRIC

SUPPLIES

ANGELUS 2-SOFT PAINT
CUP / PALETTE
PAINTBRUSH

You have to be meticulous to paint on suede or fabric! As opposed to leather, you can't remove a spot with solvent from either of them. When paint is applied, the fabric absorbs it and you can't go back.

TIP
Fabric doesn't need to be prepped with solvent before being painted.

1 Mix your color with Angelus 2-Soft at a ratio of 50% (which means you should have the same amount of 2-Soft and paint). The 2-Soft helps the fabric stay flexible when the paint dries.

2 Start painting, gradually moving along the surface.

3 Wait until the paint has dried to see whether it's been applied well and evenly. If you see areas that are lighter than the rest, go over them again and repeat the process until the area is uniform. You can speed up drying with a heat gun or, if you don't have one, a hair dryer.

TIP
To protect your paint, use a waterproofing spray. Fabric doesn't need to be varnished to protect it.

MASKING YOUR SHOE

Knowing how to mask your shoe means knowing how to protect it properly.

> **TIP**
> I use two types of tape based on the area to be masked—paper tape and vinyl tape.

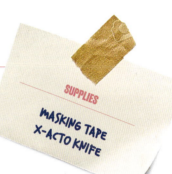

SUPPLIES
MASKING TAPE
X-ACTO KNIFE

MASKING A SOLE

1 Start by applying vinyl tape to mask the top of the sole, as shown in the photo.

2 Be careful to stick the tape firmly against the edges.

3 Cover the rest of the sole with paper tape…

4 Being careful not to leave any gaps.

5 Here's what it looks like.

49

TECHNIQUES

MASKING ANY AREA

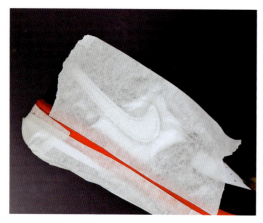

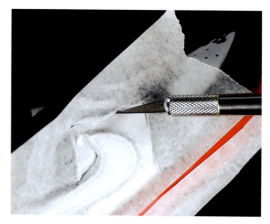

1 Stick a piece of paper tape over the area. Use enough tape that it sticks firmly to the area you want to mask.

2 With the X-Acto knife, cut off the tape all around the area to be painted, taking care to leave enough of a margin to cover the edges.

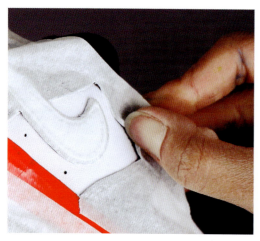

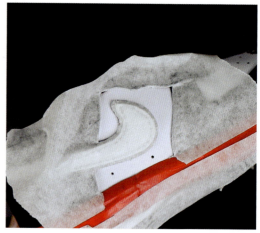

3 Remove the excess and place the margin against the edges.

4 Here's what it looks like.

TIP

If the tape is poorly placed or there are gaps, you risk getting dye underneath it. So be careful to cover the area properly, and don't forget about the edges.

MASKING THE INSIDE OF A SHOE

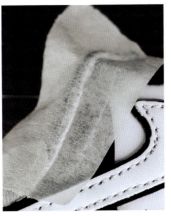

1 Stick a piece of paper tape over the area. Put enough tape on so that it sticks firmly to the area you want to mask.

2 Mark the border between the inside and the rest of the shoe with your fingernail or an object (the edge of a loyalty card, for example).

3 Using the X-Acto knife, cut along the border that you just marked.

4 Put on a second layer of tape. If you can still see the inside because there's a gap, stick some little pieces of tape on.

5 Stick more pieces of paper tape on top to cover the entire inside.

TECHNIQUES

UNSTITCHING A LOGO

SUPPLIES

X-ACTO KNIFE
TWEEZERS
PAPER TAPE

I traumatized a lot of people by cutting the Swoosh off of an Air Force 1 that I was customizing in a video (lol)! But it's helpful to remove it if you think it will get in the way of creating your design in the middle of the shoe, for example.

UNSTITCHING A SWOOSH

1 Start by cutting stitches at the tail of the Swoosh, placing the X-Acto knife against the heel.

2 Grasp the other side of the Swoosh and pull the tip up to raise it. Cut the thread under the tip.

3 Continue to cut the thread under the Swoosh by moving the tip toward the tail. Pull on the Swoosh consistently in order to keep the thread taut.

TIP

To avoid cutting or scratching the shoe, point the blade of the X-Acto knife toward the outside.

4 Remove the thread with a pair of tweezers. If any thread resists, pull on it with the tweezers in one hand and cut it off where it's attached with the X-Acto knife.

5 Here's what it looks like.

52

UNSTITCHING A PATCH

1 Using the X-Acto knife, cut the thread from above.

2 Once all the thread is cut, simply pull on the patch.

3 Remove the thread with the tweezers.

4 If there's any glue or thread remaining, use a piece of paper tape to remove it.

TIP

This approach works well on a Swoosh. It even lets you avoid scratching the shoe since you're no longer cutting the thread under the Swoosh with the X-Acto knife but rather on top of it.

TECHNIQUES

MAKING STENCILS

I'm recommending two different techniques for making stencils here. It's up to you whether you're comfortable enough with cutting your stencil directly on the shoe with the X-Acto knife (which risks scratching it) or whether you'd rather cut it out separately.

SUPPLIES

PAPER TAPE
ERASER
TOOTHBRUSH
X-ACTO KNIFE
SMARTPHONE/ TABLET

TECHNIQUE 1: NOT ON THE SHOE

1 To start, you'll need the shape you want to make a stencil of. You can draw the shape yourself or you can copy an image you've found on the internet. To demonstrate this technique, I found an image of a lightning bolt.

2 On your screen, make the image the size of the stencil you want.

4 Trace over the outline of the shape with a pencil.

3 Put your tape over the screen so that you can use it as tracing paper. You don't need to tape it on.

5 Remove the tape and stick it onto a surface to cut it.

54

TECHNIQUES

6 Using the X-Acto knife, cut out the shape following its outline. You can use a ruler to make sure you cut the lines straight.

7 Pull the tape off and stick the stencil you made where you want it on the shoe.

8 Erase the pencil marks left on the tape and carefully brush off any bits left by the eraser with a clean toothbrush.

9 Paint it in several layers using the technique for flat surfaces (see "Flat Surfaces," p. 59).

10 Remove the tape and then correct mistakes or drips if necessary.

11 Here's what it looks like.

TECHNIQUE 2: ON THE SHOE

1 Draw the shape of the stencil on your shoe freehand or by using the tracing technique (see "Drawing without Knowing How to Draw" on the next page).

2 Stick the paper tape on the shape, flattening it.

3 Using the X-Acto knife, cut the shape following its outline. Be careful not to scratch the shoe.

4 Pull off the stencil.

5 Erase any pencil marks on the shoe...

6 And carefully brush off any bits left by the eraser with a clean toothbrush.

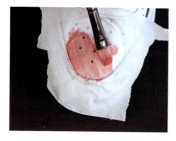
7 Paint using the technique for flat surfaces (see "Flat Surfaces," p. 59).

8 Once you've removed the tape, correct mistakes and drips if necessary.

9 Here's what it looks like.

DRAWING WITHOUT KNOWING HOW TO DRAW

It isn't rocket science! You just have to use tracing paper to be able to copy any pattern, shape, or design.

SUPPLIES

TRACING PAPER
PENCIL
SMARTPHONE/TABLET
SCISSORS
PAPER TAPE

TECHNIQUES

TIP
Before painting on leather, it's essential that you prep the surface by deglazing it. If you don't, the paint won't stick and you'll have painted for nothing (see "Prep," p. 40).

1 Put the tracing paper over the area you want to draw on and trace the border of the area to show the size of the design.

2 For this example, I found a very simple drawing of a crown. But you can use absolutely anything you'd like!

TECHNIQUES

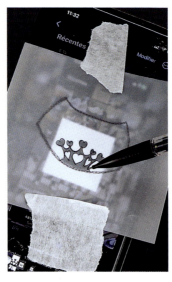

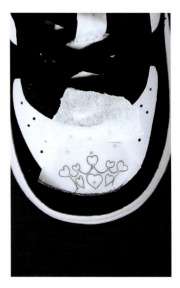

3 Adjust the size of the image on your screen to fit in the area you marked. Very important: orient the design horizontally so that the tracing will work!

4 Trace the outline of your design.

5 Cut out your design and stick it onto the chosen area with a small piece of tape.

> **TIP**
> Be careful not to move the tracing paper during this step.

6 Go over the outline of the design with your pencil.

7 Since my crown is very small, I painted it with a toothpick (see "Painting with a Toothpick," p. 68).

8 Here's what it looks like.

58

FLAT SURFACES

By flat surfaces, I mean smooth surfaces in only one color.

SUPPLIES
FLAT PAINTBRUSH
PAINT
PALETTE

> **TIP**
>
> Before painting on leather, it's essential that you prep the surface by deglazing it. If you don't, the paint won't stick and you'll have painted for nothing (see "Prep," p. 40). Choose a paintbrush that's the right size for the surface you want to fill.

1 It's best to make intermediate shades of your color by blending it with white paint so that it's uniform. Here's an example. I made two colors, one very light that I got by adding a lot of white and an intermediate one that I got with less white. I didn't mix the third one with white at all since it's the color I want to end up with.

2 Begin by mixing a tiny bit of your color with white, as in the photo.

3 You'll get a very light shade. It isn't worth putting too much paint on your brush—just on the tip is enough.

> **TIP**
> Spread the paint well. Don't let it smudge.

4 Paint your first coat, spreading the color nicely.

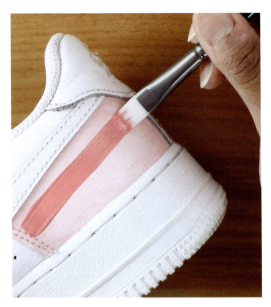

5 Wait 10-15 minutes for the paint to dry before applying a new coat. You can use a heat gun to speed up drying. Paint your second coat with your intermediate shade.

6 Wait for the paint to dry properly. It shouldn't be tacky to the touch. Last, apply a coat of paint in your original color (without mixing it with white).

7 Finish with 2-3 coats of varnish.

MAKING A SPLASH

You'll get different kinds of splashes depending on the tools you use. Splattering paint with a toothbrush gives you little spots like a starry sky, whereas splattering it with your fingers makes it go all over the place. And splattering with a paintbrush will give you spots in a line.

SUPPLIES
TOOTHBRUSH
PAINTBRUSH
SOMETHING TO PROTECT YOUR WORKSPACE (CARDBOARD BOX, TARP, ETC.)
GLOVES
PAINT

WITH A TOOTHBRUSH

TIP

As a precaution, first splatter onto your cardboard box to keep excess paint from dripping on your shoe.

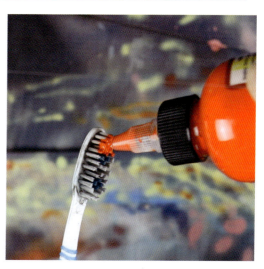

1 Before doing anything, think about protecting your workspace. I always use the same cardboard box.

2 Put some paint on the tip of the toothbrush, as in the photo. There's no need to cover the whole head of the toothbrush. You can also dip the toothbrush directly into the paint.

TECHNIQUES

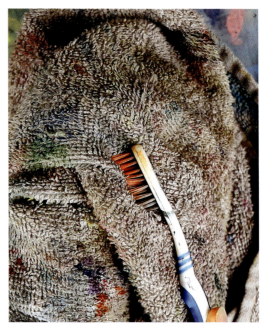

3 Using your finger, splatter the paint from the toothbrush from about 10-15 cm (4-6 inches) away from your shoe.

4 Wipe the toothbrush with a towel between each color.

5 Start the process again with a color of your choice.

6 Let the paint dry well. You can use a heat gun to speed up drying or, if you don't have one, a hair dryer.

WITH YOUR FINGERS

1 Before doing anything, think about protecting your workspace. I always use the same cardboard box.

2 Put a glove on one hand (I'm right-handed, so it's my right hand).

3 Put some paint on the tips of your fingers, as in the photo. There's no need to use too much.

4 Splatter the paint by opening and closing your hand (as in the photo) from about 10–15 cm (4–6 inches) away from the surface. Use large enough movements to splatter the paint.

5 A single splatter will give you a result as in the photo. If not, it's because you didn't have enough paint on your fingers. Add it gradually.

6 Change your glove between each color.

> **TIP**
>
> As a precaution, first splatter on your cardboard box to keep excess paint from dripping on your surface.

7 Start the process again with a color of your choice.

8 Let the paint dry well. You can use a heat gun to speed up drying or, if you don't have one, a hair dryer.

WITH A PAINTBRUSH

1 Before doing anything, think about protecting your workspace. I always use the same cardboard box.

2 Choose the size of your paintbrush based on the size you want the splatters to be.

3 Soak the handle of your paintbrush in your paint. Try not to use too much.

4 Spray the paint with your brush from about 10–15 cm (4–6 inches) away from the surface. (Think of a magic wand to cast a spell.)

5 A single spray will give you a result as in the photo. If it doesn't, that's because you didn't have enough paint on your paintbrush. Add it gradually.

TIP
As a precaution, first splatter on your cardboard box to keep excess paint from dripping on your surface.

 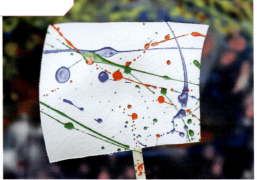

6 Wipe your paintbrush on a towel between each color.

7 Start the process again with the color of your choice. Let the paint dry well. You can use a heat gun to speed up drying or, if you don't have one, a hair dryer.

64

MAKING A "MARBLE" EFFECT

This technique works as well on leather as on fabric.

TECHNIQUES

SUPPLIES
WATER
FLAT PAINTBRUSH
FINE PAINTBRUSH
PAINT

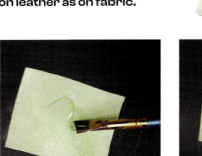
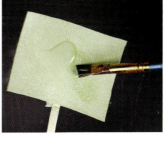

1 Start by painting the flat surface that will be the background for the "marble" effect. To get the color of the flat surface, I mixed white with the color of my "marble," green (see "Flat Surfaces," p. 59).

2 Clean your paintbrush, then slightly wet it with water and make puddles of water with it. (You can't see it in the photo very well, but I sprinkled water in several places.) There needs to be enough water for the "marble" effect to work.

3 Don't wait for the water to dry. Touch each puddle with the tip of your paintbrush, as in the photo.

TIP
Before painting on leather, it's essential that you prep the surface by deglazing it. If you don't, the paint won't stick and you'll have painted for nothing (see "Prep," p. 40).

4 Here's what happens: the paint gets diluted unevenly by the water.

5 Repeat the step with a darker shade of your color.

6 Go over the shades of color so that they pop. With a very fine paintbrush, draw some little cracks.

65

TECHNIQUES

DYEING WITH COFFEE

I love this technique! For me, it embodies the following sentence perfectly: there are really no rules limiting the techniques you can use to customize sneakers.

SUPPLIES
- INSTANT COFFEE (INTENSITY LEVEL 8 OR MORE)
- ACETONE
- COTTON PADS
- COTTON SWABS
- VERY HOT WATER
- TOWEL
- HEAVY OBJECT

1 Remove the laces and insole.

> **TIP**
> If you don't do this step properly, the dye won't last.

2 Prep the surfaces for dyeing by deglazing them with an acetone-soaked cotton pad (see "Prep," p. 40). I wanted to dye just the white parts, so I prepped only those: here, that's the sole, middle, Swoosh, and toe box.

> **TIP**
> For the dye to work, the water has to be very hot but not boiling. When you pour the water into the container, it will no longer be almost boiling and thus it will be exactly the right temperature.

3 Warm the water until it's almost boiling and pour it into a container. There needs to be enough water to cover the shoe completely.

66

4 Pour the instant coffee into the water.

5 Mix well for about 10-20 seconds.

6 Immerse your shoe completely in the mixture.

7 I use a large stone to keep the shoe from rising back to the surface (but you can use any heavy object that you aren't worried about dyeing!).

8 Wait 30 seconds.

9 Rinse the shoe in lukewarm water immediately after you take it out of the water.

> **TIP**
> If the dye didn't take in certain areas, it's because you didn't prep the surface properly with acetone. With a cotton pad or a cotton swab soaked with acetone, rub over these areas and immerse the shoe in the dye again. Rinse it in water and wash it with soap, as in the previous steps.

10 Clean your shoe by lathering it with soap to remove the coffee odor. No worries: the soap won't take away the dye! Rinse it with lukewarm water.

11 Let your shoes dry completely. You don't really need to varnish the dye, but I still recommend using a waterproof spray on it. And if the shoes still smell a little like coffee, that's normal. It will go away in time.

TECHNIQUES

PAINTING WITH A TOOTHPICK

Well, yeah! Making custom sneakers means being creative. And being creative means knowing how to use what you have on hand. A simple toothpick will let you accomplish what you have trouble doing with a paintbrush, like painting tiny details!

SUPPLIES

TOOTHPICKS
PAINT
EXTRA-FINE SANDPAPER
(400 GRIT OR HIGHER)

FOR TINY DETAILS

> **TIP**
> Before painting on leather, it's essential that you prep the surface by deglazing it. If you don't, the paint won't stick and you'll have painted for nothing (see "Prep," p. 40).

1 Equip yourself with your best box of toothpicks.

2 Using extra-fine sandpaper, sharpen the tip of one or two toothpicks. Sharpened toothpicks will let you paint more precisely since they're thinner.

> **TIP**
> In order to paint easily, your paint must be liquified enough. If it isn't applying well, add a drop of water.

3 Try not to put too much paint on your toothpick, although you'll need to dip it back into the paint often.

4 I made my pattern using both normal and sharpened toothpicks.

68

CORRECTING A MISTAKE

Very useful for fixing all the little mistakes, drips, and gaps one by one.

ON THE EDGES

Very useful for painting the outline of a Swoosh or the border of a section.

TECHNIQUES

CUSTOMIZING WITH
ACCESSORIES

Adding accessories is perhaps the easiest and oldest way to personalize your sneakers.

SUPPLIES

LACES
PINS
BEADS
BADGES

ACCESSORIES
The easiest and quickest way to personalize shoes is to add accessories!

TECHNIQUES

Choose the materials you want to customize with (whatever you want!) and have fun making sneakers that look like you!

TIP

If you want stylish laces, run over to Sweetlaces! It's a French brand that sells durable laces in different lengths and colors. My fav? "In Love."

ZOOM IN ON

THE BIG LACES FASHION?

When sneakers were increasingly becoming the ultimate accessory in the 1980s, you needed to stand out by displaying your own style. For young people then who didn't have much money and thus often owned only a single pair of sneakers, laces let them be creative. Hence the trend toward big laces and their "out-there" aspect. The hack if you couldn't find any? Using the tip of an iron to widen and flatten regular shoelaces!

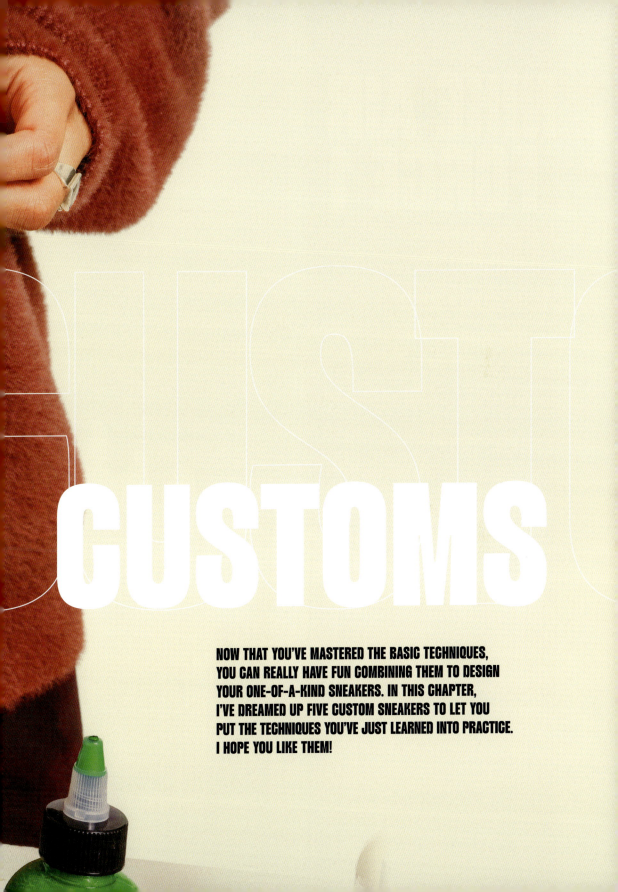

CUSTOMS

NOW THAT YOU'VE MASTERED THE BASIC TECHNIQUES, YOU CAN REALLY HAVE FUN COMBINING THEM TO DESIGN YOUR ONE-OF-A-KIND SNEAKERS. IN THIS CHAPTER, I'VE DREAMED UP FIVE CUSTOM SNEAKERS TO LET YOU PUT THE TECHNIQUES YOU'VE JUST LEARNED INTO PRACTICE. I HOPE YOU LIKE THEM!

CUSTOMS

NIKE AIR FORCE 1
"ENERGY"

I loved making this sneaker! I wanted a neutral-enough color scheme to be able to wear them easily, but the flames and the red Swoosh give them just the right character they need. If you want to adapt my custom sneaker for yourself, you can always change the color of the Swooshes. I think blue or orange would do the job nicely ;).

CUSTOMS

TECHNIQUES

To master the techniques used for this custom sneaker, refer to the following pages:

- "Prep," p. 40
- "Masking Your Shoe," p. 49
- "Making Stencils," p. 54
- "Flat Surfaces," p. 59
- "Painting with a Toothpick," p. 68
- "Varnish," p. 41

SUPPLIES

ACETONE
COTTON PADS
COTTON SWABS
VINYL TAPE
PAPER TAPE
SCISSORS
X-ACTO KNIFE
ANGELUS PAINTS:
CREAM, RED, BROWN, SAND
FLAT PAINTBRUSH
ROUND PAINTBRUSH
TOOTHPICKS
ANGELUS 2-SOFT
OR A LITTLE WATER
BLACK LACES

CUSTOMS

1 Remove the laces

> ⚠ Caution: This is a hazardous product. Wearing a mask is mandatory. Work in a well-ventilated room. Handle with care. Prohibited for children.

2 Prep the upper but not the tongue by deglazing with a cotton pad soaked with acetone (see "Prep," p. 40).

3 For seams and hard-to-reach spots, rub with a cotton swab soaked with acetone.

4 Cut some pieces of vinyl tape to mask the upper part of the sole. Mask the rest of the sole with paper tape. Stick the tape on firmly so that you don't leave any gaps (see "Masking Your Shoe," p. 49).

5 Begin by applying the Angelus Cream color on the upper minus the tongue and the inside of the Swoosh, using the technique for flat surfaces (see "Flat Surfaces," p. 59). Apply 3–5 coats to get an opaque, even finish. Don't forget to paint the edges and seams.

6 To make the flames on this custom sneaker, I used two different stenciling methods. Refer to pp. 54–56 to learn how to use these techniques.

1st Technique: If you're comfortable, you can cut out your stencil directly on the shoe. Once the paint has dried well, stick a piece of paper tape on the toe box. Completely flatten the tape at the edges as in the photo.

7 Draw the flame pattern with a pencil.

8 Cut out the pattern with your X-Acto knife, following its outline.

9 Remove the part to be painted.

10 2nd technique: Stick a piece of paper tape on the middle. Press firmly, so that the tape takes the shape of the raised section (also called a "relief").

TIPS

- Press the tape firmly to keep the paint from getting underneath.
- To avoid pulling the paint off with the tape when you remove it, stick the tape onto a piece of clothing or a table several times before applying it to your shoe so that it will be less sticky.

11 Draw your flame pattern with a pencil.

12 Remove the tape, being careful not to tear it.

13 Stick the tape on your cutting mat and cut out your pattern with the X-Acto knife following its outline and the shape of the raised section, as in the photo.

14 Put the stencil back on, matching the shapes of the raised section.

15 Using the flat paintbrush, paint the area that's outside the stencil with the brown paint made from mixing the Brown and Sand colors. If you're comfortable, you can paint the Brown directly without protecting the parts that you don't want to paint. If not, refer to the technique for "Masking Your Shoe," p. 49.

CUSTOMS

16 Use a fine, round paintbrush for tricky spots.

17 Make shadows like those in the photos by using the Brown color and a fine, round paintbrush.

18 Paint the inside of the Swooshes with the Red color. Red doesn't cover well, so begin by lightening it with white and then apply it coat by coat, darkening it gradually until you reach the original red (see "Flat Surfaces," p. 59).

19 Make shadows like those in the photos by mixing the Brown and Red colors and using a fine, round paintbrush.

20 With a flat paintbrush, paint the heel with the Black color.

21 Use a smaller paintbrush for the edges. If you're afraid of going over the edge, mask your shoe.

> **TIP**
> Angle the small paintbrush as in the photo to keep from getting the paint onto the other colors.

CUSTOMS

22 Remove the tape you used for the stencil.

23 Use a toothpick to paint the narrow edges…

24 And to fix little mistakes, as in the photo.

25 Finish by painting the label. To protect the tongue, use a piece of paper tape folded in half …

26 And slide it under the label.

27 To help the fabric absorb the paint better, dilute it by 50% with 2-Soft (or with two drops of water if you don't have that). Paint with a flat brush.

28 Varnish all painted areas with a flat brush (see "Varnish," p. 41). And I accessorized these custom sneakers with black laces to finish them.

CUSTOMS

CONVERSE CHUCK TAYLOR ALL STAR

"GRAFFITI"

This model consists of lots of little drawings. So get your inspiration from my model but use your own ideas. Customizing is the art of personalization. Feel free to express your creativity!

TECHNIQUES

To master the techniques used for this custom sneaker, refer to the following pages:

- "Painting on Fabric," p. 48
- "Unstitching a Logo," p. 52

SUPPLIES

ACETONE
X-ACTO KNIFE
TWEEZERS
PAPER TAPE
ANGELUS PAINT: LIGHT BLUE, BLACK
ANGELUS 2-SOFT
ROUND PAINTBRUSH
FLAT PAINTBRUSH

CUSTOMS

CUSTOMS

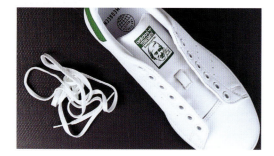

1 Remove the laces.

2 Using the X-Acto knife, cut the thread in the patch.

3 Pull on the patch so that it comes off the fabric.

4 With the tweezers, remove the remaining thread.

5 Use a piece of paper tape to pull off the adhesive that was under the patch. Repeat as necessary until there's no trace left of either the glue or the thread.

6 For the following steps, you can copy my drawings, but feel free to create your own too! Start by painting with your lightest color. I used Angelus Light Blue, which I diluted by 50% with Angelus 2-Soft to make it more liquid and so that it would adhere to the fabric better (see "Painting on Fabric," p. 48).

> **TIP**
> Use a hair dryer (or a heat gun) to make the paint dry faster between each coat.

7 Use the flat brush to fill in the drawings.

8 Once the blue is completely dry, use a fine, round brush to make the black drawings. I used Angelus Black, which I diluted by 50% with Angelus 2-Soft. I used the same brush for all the different line thicknesses, but you can use paintbrushes in different sizes.

CUSTOMS

CUSTOMS

ADIDAS STAN SMITH
"FLOWER"

To be honest, I'm not a huge fan of Stan Smiths. But what's really cool with custom sneakers is that you can make shoes your own. Here the coffee-dyed sole gives the shoes a bit of a vintage look, which is enough to make me love these Stans! I chose flowers for the designs, but you can easily change them and give them the design you want. So get your paintbrushes and, above all, let your imagination run wild!

CUSTOMS

TECHNIQUES

To master the techniques used for this custom sneaker, refer to the following pages:

- "Prep," p. 40
- "Masking Your Shoe," p. 49
- "Drawing without Knowing How to Draw," p. 57
- "Flat Surfaces," p. 59
- "Dyeing with Coffee," p. 66
- "Varnish," p. 41

SUPPLIES

ACETONE
COTTON PADS
VINYL TAPE
SCISSORS
INSTANT COFFEE
CONTAINER
VERY HOT WATER
ANGELUS PAINTS:
FLAT WHITE, PINK, RED, YELLOW, LIGHT BLUE
FLAT PAINTBRUSH
ROUND PAINTBRUSH
LEAD PENCIL
TOOTHPICK

CUSTOMS

1 Remove the laces…

2 And the insole.

3 Prep the sole and the upper, deglazing with a cotton pad soaked with acetone (see "Prep," p. 40).

4 Mask the lower part of the upper using the tape. This step is essential so that the dye for the sole doesn't stain the rest of the shoe.

5 Cut and stick many little pieces of tape on the toe box, so that each piece lies completely flat.

> **TIP**
> Use a hair dryer or a heat gun to make sure the tape is firmly attached and smooth.

6 To dye the sole with coffee (see "Dyeing with Coffee," p. 66), begin by pouring boiling water into a container large enough to hold a shoe.

CUSTOMS

TIP

For the dye to work, the water must be very, very hot but not boiling. But by pouring the water into the container, it will no longer be almost boiling and instead it will be exactly the right temperature.

7 Use enough water to completely cover the sole.

8 Pour the instant coffee into the water.

9 Mix well for around 10–20 seconds.

10 Immerse the sole completely in the mixture. Keep it in the water for 10 minutes. You can use any object to hold it there as long as the sole remains entirely in the water.

TIPS

• If your shoes smell a little like coffee, that's normal. It will go away in time.

• If the dye didn't take in certain areas, it's because you didn't prep the surface properly with acetone. Using an acetone-soaked cotton pad or cotton swab, rub over these areas and immerse the shoe in the dye again.

11 Clean your shoe with lukewarm water right away and then lather it with soap to remove the coffee odor. Don't worry: the soap won't take away the dye!

12 Dry your shoe with a cloth. If necessary, use the Flat White color and a flat paintbrush to whiten the areas where the dye got smudged.

CUSTOMS

13 Draw the patterns freehand with a pencil or use the tracing technique (see "Drawing without Knowing How to Draw," p. 57). Don't press too hard with your pencil. The marks should be barely visible.

14 Paint color by color, beginning with the lightest color. I painted in the following order: yellow, pink, red, and green.

> **TIP**
> What's the difference between White and Flat White? Flat White is White mixed with a mattifying agent. It's useful because it doesn't shine, unlike White, so it's closer to the original white of the shoes.

15 To get a finish with opaque, uniform colors, use the flat surface technique for each of the colors (see "Flat Surfaces," p. 59). Wait for the paint to dry completely between each coat.

16 Using the round paintbrush, finish with the green and red circles in the flowers.

> **TIP**
> Painting color by color means starting by doing all the yellow flowers, then all the pink flowers, and finally all the red flowers. It will save you time—you'll see!

17 To remove paint from the eyelets, you can simply scrape them with a toothpick.

18 To finish, varnish all the painted parts with the flat paintbrush (see "Varnish," p. 41).

CUSTOMS

AIR JORDAN 1
"CARTOON"

This sneaker will help you understand the importance of proceeding logically when making a custom sneaker. You'll see that if you do so, you'll go twice as fast. Before undertaking each step, I recommend you read it in its entirety to get the big picture of what you'll need to do. And to understand how to proceed, take the time to refer to the pages with the techniques you'll use.

CUSTOMS

TECHNIQUES

To master the techniques used for this custom sneaker, refer to the following pages:

"Prep," p. 40

"Painting on Fabric," p. 48

"Masking Your Shoe," p. 49

"Flat Surfaces," p. 59

"Making a Splash," p. 61

"Painting with a Toothpick," p. 68

"Varnish," p. 41

SUPPLIES

ACETONE
COTTON PAD
COTTON SWAB
VINYL TAPE
PAPER TAPE
SCISSORS
TOOTHBRUSH
ANGELUS PAINTS:
NATURAL, BLUE, YELLOW, GRAY TAUPE, SAND, BLACK, CHOCOLATE, PALE BLUE, LIGHT GRAY, WHITE
ANGELUS 2-SOFT
FLAT PAINTBRUSH
ROUND PAINTBRUSH
TOOTHPICK

CUSTOMS

1 Remove the laces.

2 Prep the upper minus the tongue by deglazing it with a cotton pad soaked with acetone (see "Prep," p. 40).

3 For hard-to-reach spots and seams, use a cotton swab soaked with acetone.

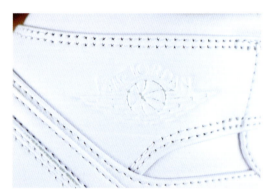

4 For the "Air Jordan" logo, you need to rub until you've completely removed the white plastic and the original white paint has peeled off a little, as in the photo.

5 Mask the upper part of the sole with the vinyl tape.

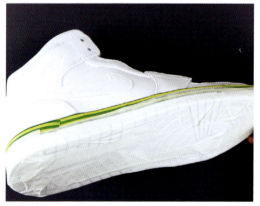

6 Mask the rest of the sole with the paper tape. Press the tape firmly and don't leave any gaps (see "Masking Your Shoe," p. 49).

> **TIP**
>
> For the following steps, the order of painting the different colors is based on the fact that you can cover a light color with a darker one. Therefore, I recommend you paint with the lightest to the darkest color and intentionally let your light colors spread over the lines. That way you'll save time by not having to sweat over details you'll cover anyway.

7 Start by painting the Natural color on the toe box, middle, and heel counter, following the technique for flat surfaces (see "Flat Surfaces," p. 59). Use your flat paintbrush to paint large areas and a fine, round paintbrush for corners and trickier spots.

8 Apply your color adequately, without wasting time worrying about it flowing onto the other parts you're going to paint. Apply 3-5 coats for an even, opaque finish.

9 Repeat the process for the blue on the mudguard and eyelets. I got this color by mixing Pale Blue, Light Gray, and White.

10 Repeat the process for the green on the heel and heel counter. I got this color by mixing Blue, Yellow, Gray Taupe, and Sand.

11 Apply the Chocolate color on the small part of the heel counter. Use a small, flat paintbrush to get a nice flat surface and to paint under the edges.

CUSTOMS

> **TIP**
>
> To avoid pulling the paint off with the tape when you remove it, stick the tape onto a piece of clothing or a table several times before applying it to your shoe so that it will be less sticky.

12 To make splatters (see "Making a Splash," p. 61), start by masking the shoe, leaving only the blue parts visible.

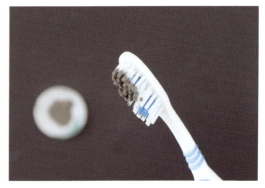

13 Don't forget to mask the tongue and the inside of the shoe. The splatters go in all directions and spots appear quickly.

14 I used the Gray Taupe color and put a small amount on my toothbrush.

> **TIP**
>
> It should look like a mummy.

15 In a protected area (I do my splatters in a cut-up cardboard box, but you can use other kinds of protective materials), make little splatters with your toothbrush. Repeat the splatter process on the green parts.

16 This stage is the trickiest because unlike other colors, you can't go over black to cover it up. Using a round brush and the Black color, paint all the edges.

17 Use the tip of the paintbrush or a toothpick for tight spaces and difficult spots.

18 To make the black bands on the Swooshes, start by cutting three pieces of tape: two the same size and one that's longer.

19 Put your three pieces of tape on the Swoosh, as in the photo.

TIP

To keep the paint from getting under the tape, press on it firmly and warm it so that it sticks better. If you don't have a heat gun, I recommend you use a hair dryer.

20 Apply the black paint with a small brush and wait for it to dry before removing the adhesive.

21 To paint the stitches along the sole, I slightly diluted the Black color with one or two drops of water so that I could apply it more easily.

22 If you get paint onto the sole, don't worry! You can easily correct it by scratching it off with a toothpick.

23 Use a toothpick to correct any small mistakes like the ones in the photo (see "Correcting a Mistake," p. 69).

24 To paint a fabric tongue (see "Painting on Fabric," p. 48), dilute a little of the Chocolate color with the same amount of 2-Soft. Blend well and paint with a flat paintbrush.

25 Varnish all the painted sections with a flat paintbrush (see "Varnish," p. 41).

CUSTOMS

NEW BALANCE 574 "COLOR"

I really like this custom sneaker, because it uses a technique that looks "Wow!" but is actually very easy to do. The real difficulty is that unlike leather, you can't remove spots from fabric. Just one wrong move and things can quickly become a mess! So take your time practicing before tackling this sneaker but, above all, trust yourself!

CUSTOMS

TECHNIQUES

To master the techniques used for this custom sneaker, refer to the following pages:

"Prep," p. 40

"Painting on Fabric," p. 48

"Making a 'Marble' Effect," p. 65

"Flat Surfaces," p. 59

"Varnish," p. 41

SUPPLIES

ANGELUS PAINTS: BROWN, WHITE, BLACK, NATURAL, BEIGE, RED, ORANGE, GOLD, OLIVE, SAND

ANGELUS 2-SOFT ROUND PAINTBRUSH

FLAT PAINTBRUSH

WATER

ACETONE

COTTON PAD

COTTON SWAB

CUSTOMS

1 Remove the laces.

2 Prep the leather parts by deglazing with a cotton pad soaked with acetone (see "Prep," p. 40).

> ⚠ Caution: This is a hazardous product. Wearing a mask is mandatory. Work in a well-ventilated room. Handle with care. Prohibited for children.

3 For tricky-to-reach spots and seams, use a cotton swab soaked with acetone.

4 Paint the small leather portion with a flat paintbrush. I got a very light brown by mixing the White color with a tiny bit of Brown (very little). Use a smaller paintbrush and a round paintbrush for the spots where you're worried about going over the edges.

5 To paint the area in the middle, blend the Natural, Beige, and Brown colors. Add 50% Angelus 2-Soft to the blend. Your mixture should permeate the fabric without making it stiff.

6 Apply the mixture with a flat paintbrush. Use a round paintbrush for the edges.

8 Dab your flat paintbrush into the water and make puddles (the water isn't visible in the photo, but I sprinkled it over several places on the N). There has to be enough water for the "marble" effect to work.

7 Now we've reached the really interesting step for this sneaker! Start by applying two thin coats of a blend of White with a tiny bit of Red. You'll end up with kind of a light pink that will be the base for the "marble" effect (see "Making a 'Marble' Effect," p. 65).

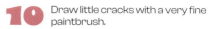

CUSTOMS

9 Don't wait for the water to dry. Touch each puddle with the tip of your paintbrush using shades of red, as in the photo. Go over the red spots so that the colors stand out nicely.

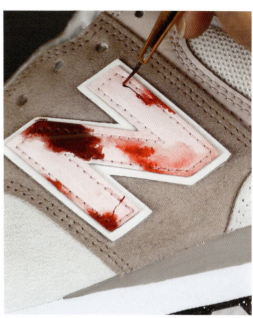

10 Draw little cracks with a very fine paintbrush.

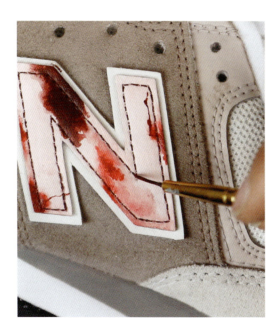

11 Go over the topstitching with a dark red to give the N a finished look.

12 Repeat the marbling process on the heel and mudguard with green. Be careful! The parts here are suede, so you'll use the technique for fabric (see "Making a 'Marble' Effect," p. 65). I used Angelus colors Olive, Sand, and Black.

CUSTOMS

13 You can paint the inside borders as in the photos, which will give a finished look. But be careful not to go over them!

14 To finish this custom sneaker, I painted a mix of Orange and Gold on the label...

15 And the tongue.

16 All that's left is to varnish the leather parts.

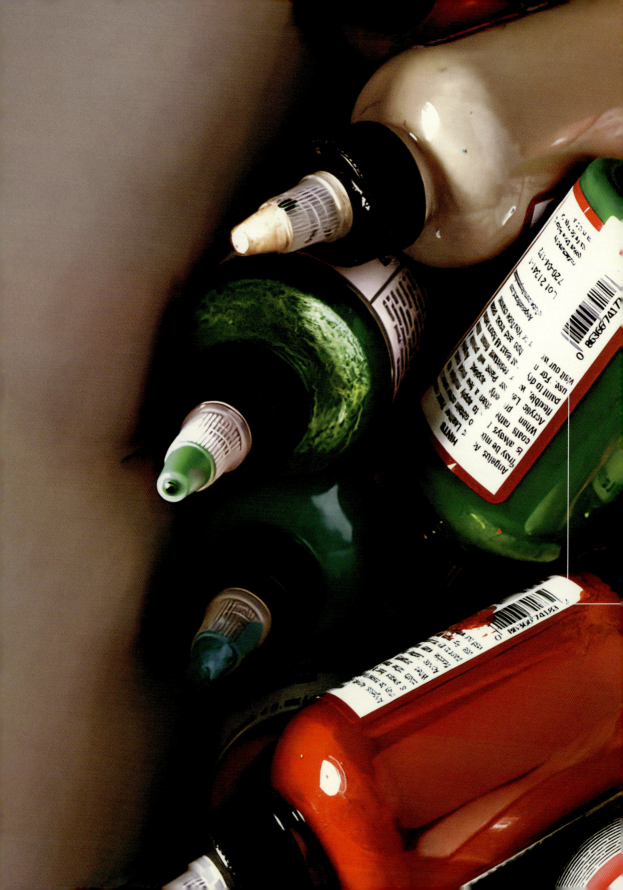

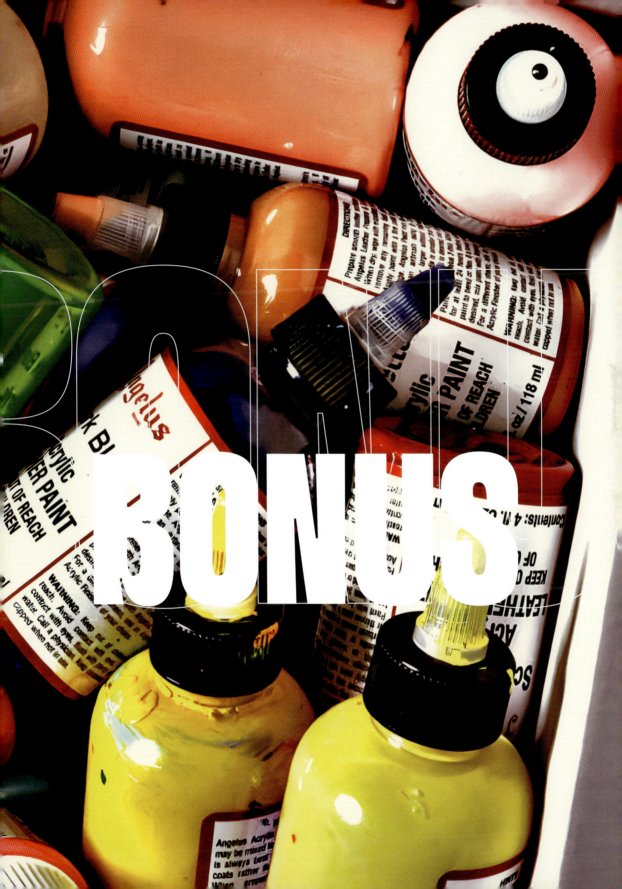

BONUS

TOOLS TO DIG DEEPER

I hope *Custom Sneakers* has made you want to continue your adventure in the world of customizing! The tools I'll show you here are more expensive and more complicated to master, which is why I don't think they're appropriate for beginners. But for those who have mastered the basics of customizing sneakers and want to keep going, here's a list of tools, resources, and advice to help you get to the next level!

AIRBRUSH

I can't wait to tell you about this magic tool that has completely changed how I customize. The airbrush is paired with its (noisy) companion, the air compressor. Together they've allowed me to create much more advanced custom sneakers. An airbrush is a small gun the size of a pen that lets you spray paint using compressed air. An air compressor is a device connected to the airbrush by a cord; it compresses air.

This tool lets you:
Paint flat surfaces in record time
- Make gradients
- Fill in stencils more accurately
- Create highlighting and neon effects
- Apply varnish or finisher more evenly

You'll find more information and templates at www.knz-custom.fr.

CUTTING MACHINE

Next to an airbrush, this is the tool that catapulted my practice forward. With it you can make:
- single-use stencils
- professional-quality reusable stencils
- text, logos
- precise drawings
- cut-outs in materials such as leather

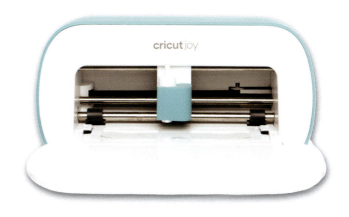

> **TIP**
> I use a Cricut Joy cutting machine.

FINISHER

This liquid product will help give your paint a uniform finish. Use it after the last coat of paint has dried completely. Apply 2-3 thin coats, letting each dry completely before applying the next one. Unlike varnish, which protects the paint, finishers just help you even out the finish.

HEAT GUN

Although a beginner doesn't need this, I highly recommend it for more regular practice.

> **TIP**
> I recommend Angelus finishers. Once they're dry, they're waterproof and flexible enough for shoes. As with varnish, they come in matte, satin, and high gloss.

DULLER

This additive lets you mattify paint, finisher, or varnish. It's well regarded among professionals because it gives a "manufactured" look to creations by minimizing the extra natural brightness in products without dimming their sheen. Be careful to add only a few drops to your paint, however. Once it's applied, the paint finish should look very dull.

TAKING CARE OF YOUR CUSTOM SNEAKERS OVER TIME

BONUS

DO

• Waterproof with a waterproofing spray: finish and increase the waterproofing that's already in the paint and the varnish.

• Rub areas that need cleaning with a soft brush, lathering with cold water and soap (preferably Marseille soap).

DON'T

• Wash your shoes in a washing machine. This may make them lose their shape as well as remove the paint.

• Scrape your shoes against stairs, the sidewalk, or the ground. This may scratch the varnish and the paint.

• Use products that are too abrasive: avoid solvents, acetone, and alcohol-based products.

• Rub with a hard brush. If the bristles are too coarse, they may scratch the varnish and the paint.

machine à laver

THE IMPACT OF CUSTOM SNEAKERS ON FASHION

DAPPER DAN'S LEGACY WITH VIRGIL ABLOH

In the early 1980s, New York designer Dapper Dan was already playing around with combining the worlds of sportswear and luxury for his clients' sneakers. Coming from hip-hop and the street, Dan's clientele weren't exactly popular with luxury brands, which is why they opted for custom sneakers. Thirty years later, the work of the late Virgil Abloh picked up this concept. Artistic director at Louis Vuitton from 2018 to 2021, he designed the 47 Nike Air Force 1 for the 2022 spring-summer men's collection in collaboration with Louis Vuitton. Coming from the world of sportswear, Abloh considered the Nike Air Force 1 an emblem and wanted to pay personal homage to the customizing culture he had grown up with by combining two opposite aesthetics.

LOUIS VUITTON NIKE AIR FORCE 1 BREAKS AN AUCTION RECORD

On February 9, 2022, at Sotheby's, 200 pairs of the same 47 Nike Air Force 1 model that Virgil Abloh designed broke an auction record, exceeding $25 million. With this sale, Sotheby's became part of the trend among the biggest auction houses to grow their streetwear departments, meeting the increasing demand of collectors younger than their regular target market.

ADIDAS X *YU-GI-OH*: CUSTOM SNEAKERS OR NOT?

On October 7, 2022, Adidas released two sneakers in collaboration with the manga series *Yu-Gi-Oh*: the Adidas ADi2000 Yu-Gi-Oh! Dark Magician and the Adidas ADi2000 Blues Eyes White Dragon. The two models got mixed reviews, but one of them stands out, as it's reminiscent of custom sneakers made with paint and a paintbrush. It should be noted that the two models are characterized by having an almost entirely white color scheme, with a simple design in the middle of the upper.

The late Virgil Abloh, Louis Vuitton artistic director from 2018 to 2021.

Nike Air Force 1 designed by Virgil Abloh for Louis Vuitton (spring-summer 2022 season)

SHOE BRANDS AND THEIR PERSONALIZATION PROGRAMS

Nike, Converse, Vans, Adidas, Timberland—all these brands offer or have offered online personalization services. Integrated into their official websites, these services let customers personalize their shoes. At Nike, this is called Nike by You (formerly NKEID) and has been around since 1999 in the US and 2001 in Europe. For a few dozen dollars extra, you can modify all the parts of a shoe by playing with the colors, the patterns, and even the materials. Personalizing at Adidas is a little more limited, as you can only add a word or a number at the top of the upper. In 2016, Timberland launched its program, which is called DYO (Design Your Own). Currently unavailable, the service lets you personalize the tiniest details on the brand's 11 iconic models.

SPOTLIGHT ON DIY AT PUMA AND CHINATOWN MARKET

In 2019, NY brand Chinatown Market joined forces with sports equipment manufacturer Puma with a DIY (Do It Yourself) collection. They

BONUS

supplied colored pieces of Velcro with four models of sneakers, which let wearers play with different options for the same shoes or exchange the Velcro between two models. Clothing and accessories filled out the collection. "It's all about giving the customer the feeling of buying not just one product, but having many different ways of mixing up their sneakers," said Mike Cherman, Chinatown Market founder, when the line was launched.

CUSTOM SNEAKERS IN RESPONSE TO COVID

In 2020, in response to the first lockdown during COVID-19, Converse launched the #CreateAtHome campaign. Geared specifically to students, it invited them to design their own Converse Chuck Taylor All Star model on paper or digitally. The campaign included a social media PR strategy, with participants asked to post their creations using the hashtag and share them with their friends. Converse also chose a handful of creative influencers to boost the campaign.

BONUS

SOS KNZ
I HAVE A PROBLEM WITH MY CUSTOM SNEAKER!

I WORE MY SHOES AND THE PAINT CAME OFF!

If the paint came off, it may be that you didn't prep the surface properly. Or perhaps you didn't allow enough time for each coat to dry or the paint wasn't applied correctly?

There are so many reasons the paint can come off that it's best to follow all the steps carefully.
- Paints to use: p. 31
- The three steps for making a custom sneaker: p. 40
- Prep your medium: p. 40
- Paint: p. 41
- Working with flat surfaces: p. 59
- Varnishing: p. 41

MY DESIGN DOESN'T LOOK LIKE THE ORIGINAL!

If you're not good at drawing, no worries! Use the tracing paper technique (p. 57).

THE MASKNG TAPE PULLED OFF MY PAINT!

There are two possibilities here. Either you didn't follow the earlier steps (prep, painting, drying, etc.) or the tape is too strong! It's best to test it on a small area. If it pulls off the paint, try making it less sticky by applying it to another surface several times before using it on your shoes.

I update my tape recommendations regularly at my website, www.knz-custom.fr.

THE VARNISH LEFT WHITE MARKS ON THE PAINT!

Make the varnish slightly more liquid by adding a few drops of water (adjust according to the amount of varnish). Let the varnish dry well between each coat. If you use a heat gun, make sure it isn't too close to the shoe (so that the excess heat doesn't affect the varnish). Also be careful that your paintbrush is completely clean and slightly damp between each coat.

I GOT A PAINT SPOT...

On my leather shoes!
You can easily fix stains on leather by wiping them with solvent. Use cotton swabs for small areas!

On my fabric shoes!
It's very hard to get a paint stain off fabric. If you haven't yet customized your shoes, you can hand-wash the whole shoe, rubbing it with warm water and Marseille soap or detergent and stain remover. If you get a paint stain on them after you've begun customizing, all you can do is adjust the design of your custom to cover the stain.

On my laces!
It's very hard to get paint off laces. That's why you should always remove them before customizing. If they get stained, rub them with warm water and hand soap. Then scrub the stain in a solution of cold water and a little bit of bleach that you've added a small amount of detergent to. Let them rest in the mixture for 30–60 minutes and then rinse the laces well in cold water.

On my soles!
You can scrape paint off rubber or plastic parts with a toothpick or any other tool that's fairly hard. Depending on the colors, solvent may also work.

MY PAINT WON'T GO ON RIGHT!

Make the paint slightly more liquid with water or 2-Soft so that it flows better. One to three drops is enough.

THE PAINT HAS SOAKED INTO THE SEAMS!

This may be because the paint is too liquid. The best thing is to keep a close eye when you get near the seams and avoid touching them directly if possible.

BONUS

INSPIRATIONS

Custom shoes are for everyone! There are as many ways to make them as there are fans.
In the next few pages, I've put together a few custom sneakers made by some of the most talented customizers and creatives I know. But respect their work: I'm counting on you not to copy their designs. Just let them inspire you!

BONUS

@BLACK_DESTINATOR_KUSTOM

@BRUNOGRAFFER

@BRUNOGRAFFER

BONUS

@kyxcustoms

@isidorestudio

@staniflow

@black_dessinator_kustom

@stamiflou

@silmi.art

@landy.t

@ISIDORESTUDIO

@KYXCUSTOMS

@LANDY.T

BONUS

@silmi.art

@flub

@black_dessinator_kustom

@staniflou

GLOSSARY

ACETONE

Solvent used to deglaze leather shoes by removing industrial varnish finishes or all other residues that would keep paint from adhering (dust, dirt, mud, etc.).

Be careful handling this product, as it's a toxic substance and hazardous to your health. Keep it out of reach of children. Wearing a mask is mandatory. Use outdoors or in a well-ventilated room.

MASKING TAPE

Sticky tape used to mask areas that shouldn't be painted. It can be made of paper or vinyl.

ADDITIVE

Liquid substance added to paint to change its characteristics. Additives allow paints that were originally intended for leather to be used on other materials, such as plastic or even fabric.

AIRBRUSH

Small paint gun the size of a pen that lets you spray paint via compressed air.

FLAT SURFACE

Surface made up of only one uniform color.

COLOR SCHEME

Set of colors in a custom sneaker, sometimes called "colorway" or "palette."

SUEDE

Specific leather finish that gives it a velvety appearance and makes it soft to the touch.

SOLVENT

Chemical product used to clean a surface. It dissolves and removes all residues that would hinder paint application, such as varnish, silicone, or dirt.
   Examples: acetone, Angelus Preparer and Deglazer.

HEAT GUN

Tool shaped like a hair dryer that projects a flow of very hot air (between 200 and 600°C or 392 and 1112°F). Generally used to deglaze paint or varnish, it makes paint on custom sneakers dry quickly.

FULL CUSTOMIZATION

Customizing all the parts of a shoe.

HIGH

Adjective describing a high-top sneaker that ends above the ankle.

LOW

Adjective describing a low-top sneaker that ends below the ankle.

MOCKUP

Depiction of what the custom shoe will look like. It can be created digitally on a computer (digital mockup) or drawn by hand (drawn mockup).

MID

Adjective describing a mid-top sneaker that ends at the ankle.

STENCIL

Printing technique and, by extension, an object that lets the same pattern be copied on a material many times, as only the cut-out sections let the pigment through.

SNEAKERS

Athletic (basketball) shoes whose function has expanded into a daily fashion accessory. The word "sneakers" comes from "to sneak," which means to move furtively and discreetly. It refers to rubber soles being quieter on the ground, in contrast to the hard soles of leather shoes, which are thus noisier.

SWOOSH

The name of the logo for the Nike brand, also commonly called "the comma" in French.

MOCKUPS FOR YOUR CUSTOM SNEAKERS

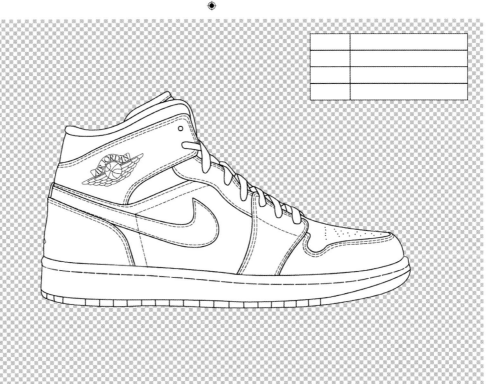

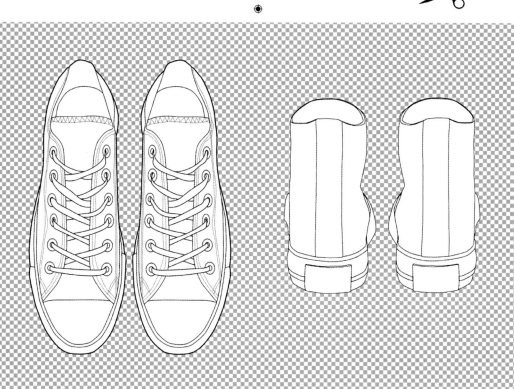

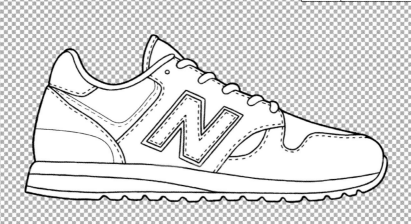

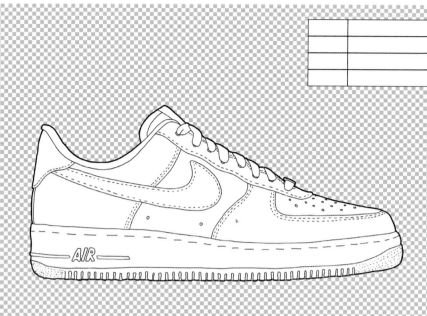
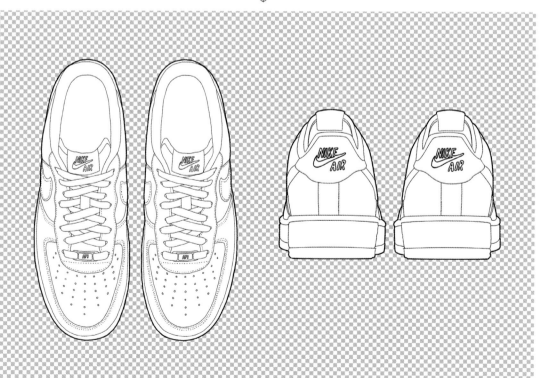

Thank you to the entire Éditions Solar team for being part of my first book and especially Corinne and Iris for supporting me in the very best way.

Thank you to Alexi Pavlov and his team for the divine photos!

Thank you to the Smile team for the help.

Thank you to my little brother Marius for illustrating the pages of this book so beautifully.

Thank you to Mom and Dad for passing on to me your love of art and a job well done.

Thank you to my friends who helped, advised, and encouraged me.

Thank you to my girlfriend, without whom I would never have managed to reach the end of this crazy adventure.

Thank you to all the custom sneaker artists who trusted me and agreed to share their talent in the inspiration pages of this book.

Thank you to Angelus as well as Pébéo for their wonderful paints.

Thank you to Cricut, which also supported my projects.

Thank you to the iconic sneaker brands (particularly Adidas, Converse, New Balance, Nike, and Vans) that have been an inexhaustible source of inspiration for my custom sneakers.

And, finally, thank you to my subscribers for their support, as well as all of you who give my work importance.

For their gracious participation in shooting, the publisher thanks:

Léa Waldberg (@leawaldberg.styliste), Victoria San Roman (@thevixx, make-up artist), and Jacques Giaume from Studio 258 (@studio258_paris).

Photography: Alexi Pavlov

All the photos are by Alexi Pavlov except:

p. 12: Alamy/ Trinity Mirror/ Mirrorpix;

p. 15: Alamy/ Mikkel Petersen; Alamy/Cristian Storto;

p. 18-19: Alamy/ Mikkel Petersen;

p. 20-21: Alamy/ xMarshall;

p. 22-23: Alamy/ Cristian Storto;

p. 24-25: Alamy/ Sergio Azenha;

p. 26-28 and p. 29 left: DR;

p. 29 right: Alamy/ xMarshall;

p. 70: Adobe Sock;

p. 71: @sweet_laces;

p. 125: Alamy/ Aurore Marechale/ PA Images;

p. 126: Alamy/ UPI;

p. 127: Alamy/ David Bokuchava;

p. 131: @black_dessinator_kustom, @brunograffer;

p. 132: @kyxcustoms, @isidorestudio, @staniflou, @black_dessinator_kustom;

p. 133: @staniflou, @landy.t, @kyxcustoms;

p. 134-35: @silni.art, @staniflou, @flub, @black_dessinator_kustom.

Custom Sneakers: Everything You Need to Personalize Your Kicks copyright © 2025 by Kenza Trasfi. Photographs © 2025 by Alexi Pav. Translated by Nanette McGuinness. Original Edition © 2024, Éditions Solar, a subsidiary of Edi8. 92, avenue de France - 75013 Paris. serviceclients @lisez.com. All rights reserved. Printed in China. No part of this book may be used or reproduced in any manner whatsoever without written permission, except in the case of reprints in the context of reviews.

Andrews McMeel Publishing
a division of Andrews McMeel Universal
1130 Walnut Street, Kansas City, Missouri 64106

www.andrewsmcmeel.com

25 26 27 28 29 TEN 10 9 8 7 6 5 4 3 2 1

ISBN: 979-8-8816-0154-6

Library of Congress Control Number: 2025930188

Andrews McMeel Publishing is committed to the responsible use of natural resources and is dedicated to understanding, measuring, and reducing the impact of our products on the natural world. By choosing this product, you are supporting responsible management of the world's forests. The FSC® label means that the materials used for this product come from well-managed FSC®-certified forests, recycled materials, and other controlled sources.

ATTENTION: SCHOOLS AND BUSINESSES
Andrews McMeel books are available at quantity discounts with bulk purchase for educational, business, or sales promotional use. For information, please email the Andrews McMeel Publishing Special Sales Department: sales@andrewsmcmeel.com.